TO:

FROM:

Published by Hallmark Gift Books,
a division of Hallmark Cards, Inc.,
Kansas City, MO 64141
Visit us on the Web at www.Hallmark.com.

Editor: Emily Osborn
Art Director: Kevin Swanson
Designer: Mark Voss
Production Artist: Bryan Ring

ISBN: 978-1-59530-362-2
BOK2115

Printed and bound in China
SEP11

NOW YOU'RE 70!

BY BRANDON CROSE

Hallmark
GIFT BOOKS

You were born during the austere and patriotic years of World War II, surviving on ration coupons, radio broadcasts, and hope. You were there when the Atomic Age began, when automobiles first crowded the streets, and when TV changed everything. You were also part of the first-ever teenage culture, coming of age amidst fallout shelters, drive-ins, and the rebellious sound of Rock 'n' Roll. The Silent Generation? Not a chance! You have quite a story to tell …

WHEN YOU WERE
BORN

IN THE NEWS

. . . .

The world was at war. Gripping reports by war correspondents
Ernie Pyle and Edward R. Murrow of German air raids on
England made many Americans reconsider their country's
isolation. The Blitz lasted for 57 consecutive nights.

An early morning Japanese air assault on the U.S. military base
in Pearl Harbor damaged or destroyed 21 ships, 341 aircraft, and
ended 2,403 American lives. "Remember Pearl Harbor" became the
rallying cry for America's entry into World War II.

On Presidential order, more than 110,000 Japanese–Americans
were relocated to one of ten internment camps, where they
endured overcrowded and poor living conditions for two and
a half years.

After receiving a troubling telegram from Switzerland, the
American Jewish Congress began holding rallies in major U.S.
cities to raise awareness of the rumored "Nazi death camps."
The Jewish death toll was thought to be over 3 million . . .
the final number was twice that.

"A day of infamy."

ATTACK ON PEARL HARBOR

EVENTS

It was a time of sweeping change: inspired by "Rosie the Riveter," several million women excelled at jobs that were traditionally male-only, helping to build the ships, tanks, planes, and guns that were needed to win the war.

For the first time, women were also allowed to join the four military branches as auxiliary support. More than 300,000 volunteered to become "soldiers in skirts"—SPARS, WASPS, WACS, and WAVES.

Even everyday Americans banded together like never before to support the war effort, from collecting millions of tons of rubber, metals, and cooking fat to donating every spare cent to buy a total of $135 billion in war bonds.

Physical therapy was born when you were! After nearly a decade of skepticism from her peers in Australia and England, Sister Elizabeth Kenny's unconventional massage treatment for infantile muscle paralysis found a warm reception in the United States.

MUSIC

• •

You may not remember now, but "Don't Sit Under the Apple Tree" by The Andrews Sisters, "When the Lights Go on Again" by Vaughn Monroe, and "Praise the Lord and Pass the Ammunition!" as performed by Kay Kyser and His Orchestra were among the first songs you ever heard.

Eleven-year-old conductor prodigy Lorin Maazel led the NBC Summer Symphony, and baby talk was the inspiration for the nonsense novelty song "Mairzy Doats," which was a surprise No. 1 hit both at home and with soldiers overseas.

Big bands were still a big deal, with Tommy and Jimmy Dorsey, Harry James, Artie Shaw, Duke Ellington, Benny Goodman, and Glenn Miller all selling top records.

MOVIES

A movie ticket was a dime (or possibly a quarter on the weekends), and admission got you two movies, newsreels of the war, an episode of a weekly serial such as *Dick Tracy vs. Crime, Inc.* or *Jungle Girl*, and a cartoon. Donald Duck starred in many of them, but his most famous was the anti-Nazi *Der Feuhrer's Face*, which won an Academy Award for "Best Short Feature."

Your parents may have seen one of the many popular war movies of the time: *Wake Island, Yankee Doodle Dandy, Gung Ho!, A Yank on the Burma Road*, and of course: *Casablanca*.

While Hollywood "went to war," many famous actors did actually go to war, including James Stewart, Frank Capra, Mickey Rooney, and Clark Gable.

Other silver screen and box office stars of the day included Bob Hope, Bette Davis, Spencer Tracy, Judy Garland, Humphrey Bogart, James Cagney, Betty Grable, and Greer Garson.

TV

Like refrigerators and stoves, the production of new television sets were banned during the war, so they were difficult to find, and expensive—a staggering $700!

Radio remained king, and your family's standards probably included FDR's "Fireside Chats," Lux Radio Theater, Ma Perkins, The Shadow, Fibber McGee and Molly, Gang Busters, and Let's Pretend with Billie Burke.

Many future television stars had successful radio shows during this time, such as Milton Berle, Jack Benny, Abbott and Costello, and Red Skelton.

NBC became the first commercial TV station, and the first-ever commercial was for the Bulova Time Signal watch.

SPORTS

. . . .

Joe "the Brown Bomber" Louis successfully defended the heavy-weight title against twenty-five contenders before enlisting as a private in the U.S. Army. The heavyweight title was frozen until his return.

Over 1,000 of America's baseball heroes also went to war after the bombing of Pearl Harbor— including "The Yankee Clipper" himself, Joe Dimaggio . . . but not before he hit in a record fifty-six straight games!

With many of baseball fans' favorite players gone, sports enthusiasts turned to college football. The 1942 Rose Bowl, typically held in Pasadena, California, was instead relocated to Durham, North Carolina, for fear of another Japanese attack. Despite the unexpected home advantage, Duke still lost to Oregon State: 20–16.

POP CULTURE

· ·

For baby boys, your parents were most likely to name you James, Robert, John, William, or Richard. For baby girls, Mary, Barbara, Patricia, Linda, and Carol were the most popular choices.

To help the war effort, the Office of Price Administration (or OPA) distributed ration coupons to every American family, including yours! Meat, canned goods, coffee, and gas quickly became precious commodities. But in the words of the Office of Civilian Defense, "Conservation is a war weapon in the hands of every man, woman, and child."

"Kilroy Was Here," but food was scarce. To offset the sudden shortage, more than 20 million families began growing "Victory Gardens." Some even purchased illegal quantities of rationed goods from friends and underground dealers.

Richard and Maurice McDonald opened the first McDonald's restaurant in San Bernardino, California.

WHEN YOU WERE
A KID

IN THE NEWS

The massive D-Day invasion at Normandy involved over 150,000 soldiers, nearly 7,000 ships, and just over 15,000 aircraft. Victory had a steep cost—by the end of the first day, an estimated 10,000 Allied soldiers were either dead or wounded.

Just twenty-five days after the headlines read "Roosevelt Dies," Germany surrendered to Allied forces. Our nation's first and only four-term president, FDR was replaced by his newly elected Vice President, Harry Truman.

If your family read the *Chicago Tribune*, you probably thought that Thomas Dewey beat Harry Truman in the 1948 Presidential election. The November 3rd issue went to press before all results were in—Truman, of course, was the victor.

A changing world: the United Nations was founded, an "iron curtain" fell across Berlin, and Chairman Mao proclaimed the People's Republic of China.

EVENTS

· ·

The invention of the atomic bomb and the subsequent annihilation of two Japanese cities, Hiroshima and Nagasaki, definitively ended the war and gave birth to an atomic age of boundless scientific achievement. Suddenly, anything was possible . . . even the end of the world.

If your father or uncle went to college after returning from the war, he didn't have to pay for it! The G.I. Bill of Rights covered all college expenses for veterans and made higher education possible for nearly 8 million Americans.

Researchers at Bell Telephone Laboratories invented the transistor, a tiny gadget that revolutionized modern electronics and eventually gave you your transistor radio!

More than 1.5 million African Americans had served in the war, and many had been promoted to officer ranks. Long-held racial divisions were breaking down, and in 1948, President Truman ordered the desegregation of the armed forces.

Gene Autry's perennial holiday favorite, "Rudolph the Red-Nosed Reindeer," hit the airwaves for the first time.

MUSIC

· ·

Some of your other favorite songs might have included
"Zip-a-Dee-Doo-Dah" from *Song of the South*, "It's Magic"
by Doris Day, and "A Bushel and a Peck" as performed by
Perry Como and Betty Hutton.

You didn't have to be a "bobby-soxer" to enjoy Frank Sinatra—
you probably grew up listening to his radio shows, and your
parents may have even owned his first studio album: The Voice
of Frank Sinatra. (It shot to the top of the Billboard chart and
remained on it for the next eighteen weeks.)

Jazz and bebop were still big, and after performing with other
legends such as Dizzy Gillespie, Miles Davis, and Fats Navarro,
Billy Eckstine became a tremendously popular solo artist, rivaling
even Frank Sinatra with hits like "Everything I Have is Yours"
and "I Apologize."

MOVIES

· ·

Other kids were winning Oscars! *A Tree Grows in Brooklyn's* Peggy Ann Garner, *The Yearling's* Claude Jarman, Jr., *The Search's* Ivan Jandl, and *The Window's* Bobby Driscoll all won Honorary Juvenile Academy Awards—a category that Shirley Temple first won in 1934.

You may have seen *It's a Wonderful Life, Miracle on 34th Street,* and Disney classics *Cinderella, Alice in Wonderland,* and *Peter Pan* when they were first in the theaters.

The Red Scare that would soon sweep the nation began with hearings by the House Un-American Activities Committee that led to the blacklisting of some of Hollywood's greatest talents, such as Charlie Chaplin, Lillian Hellman, Arthur Miller, Orson Welles, and Dorothy Parker, who famously wrote in a letter to the committee: "I cannot and will not cut my conscience to fit this year's fashions."

TV

. . . .

After the war, a movie producer predicted, "Television won't be able to hold on to any market it captures after the first six months. People will soon get tired of staring at a plywood box every night." How wrong he was—American families turned from radio to TV in greater numbers with each passing year.

You witnessed many now-familiar firsts: the wildly popular Milton Berle (or "Uncle Miltie") hosted the first-ever telethon, raising $1 million for cancer research in fourteen hours, and you also saw the first television broadcast of a World Series—the New York Yankees vs. the Brooklyn Dodgers.

Mr. Potato Head was the first toy advertised on television. The marketing paid off— the Hasbro toy raked in over $4 million during its first year. (But you had to supply your own potato.)

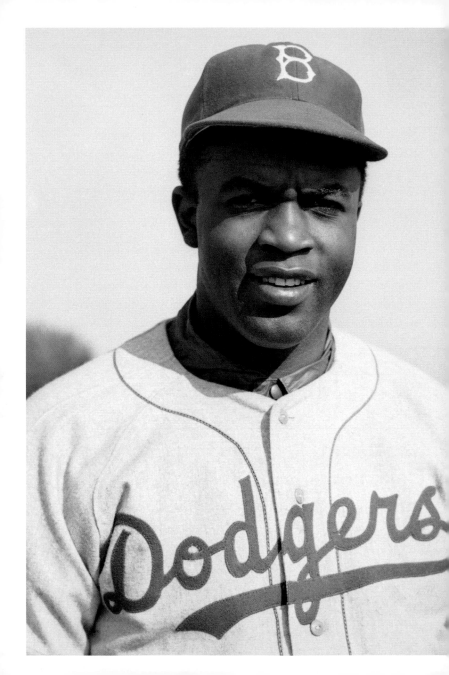

SPORTS

The Games of the XIV Olympiad (or, less formally, the 1948 Summer Olympics in London) were the first of your lifetime—due to the outbreak of war, they had been suspended since the 1936 Summer Olympics in Berlin. The United States dominated with 84 medals, 38 of them gold.

Jackie Robinson broke professional baseball's color barrier by becoming the first African American to play Major League Baseball since 1889 and then made history again by earning Rookie of the Year for his first season.

The National Basketball Association (NBA) grew out of the Basketball Association of America (BAA), with 6'10" George Mikan easily dominating those early games.

Did you hear "the shot heard 'round the world"? In the bottom of the ninth, Bobby Thomson hit a spectacular three-run home run, winning the National League pennant for the New York Giants.

POP CULTURE

Old classics such as Tinkertoys, Lincoln Logs, and Erector Sets
were still around, but now you also had Candy Land, Chutes
and Ladders, Clue, and Scrabble! New toys included Tonka Trucks.

Even if you didn't have a bicycle or clamp-on roller skates, you still
had lively neighborhood games of kick the can, red rover, work-up
softball, tag, and hide-and-seek.

Between April and September, the arrival of the Good Humor Man
with his crisp white uniform and wide array of frozen confections
probably caused a minor riot in your neighborhood. Your Good
Humor bar cost a dime . . . unless you found a "free stick" in your
last bar!

During the summer, your family may have packed up the car and
joined countless others for a new tradition: the family road trip!
During the war, you had to be on a list to buy a car, but now new
models were everywhere!

Silly Putty is "invented" during the war when a General Electric engineer tried to create a synthetic rubber.

A TEENAGER

IN THE NEWS

· ·

Senator Joseph McCarthy's wild accusations of Communist sympathizers and spies within the federal government amplified Cold War fear . . . until the Army–McCarthy hearings led to his fall from grace.

You still liked Ike: after a spate of health problems, President Eisenhower barely campaigned for his second term and handily won over Adlai Stevenson— 36 million votes to 26 million.

There were only forty-eight states until Alaska and Hawaii became the 49th and 50th in 1959 and 1960, respectively. (But you probably only wanted to vacation in one of them.)

EVENTS

· ·

The Civil Rights Movement won a major victory in Brown v.
Board of Education, with the Supreme Court ruling at last that
segregation in public schools was unconstitutional.

Scientific advancements seemed to belong more to science fiction
than reality: Sputnik I and then II circled the Earth, NASA was
born with the passing of The National Aeronautics and Space Act,
and an early test of the hydrogen bomb at Bikini Atoll was
estimated to burn five times hotter than the sun's core.

As the long-term consequences of exposure to even small amounts
of radiation became clear, 9,000 scientists from fifty countries
asked the United Nations to ban above-ground nuclear testing.

The world became a smaller place
with the invention of the jet engine.
Pan American's jet planes offered
America's first commercial trans-
atlantic flights: New York to London.

Buddy Holly, Richie Valens, and JP "The Big Bopper" Richardson met their end in a tragic plane crash.

MUSIC

· ·

Your stars included Little Richard, Jerry Lee Lewis, Bill Haley and His Comets, and the King himself: Elvis Presley, with his early hit songs "Hound Dog," "Love Me Tender," and "Heartbreak Hotel."

You might have "rocked around the clock" on 45 rpm records in your room or on your Sony TR-63 Pocket-Sized Transistor Radio or even (if you were lucky) on the radio in your car!

Other familiar songs included Chuck Berry's "Maybelline," Frankie Lyman and the Teenagers' "Why Do Fools Fall in Love," and Marty Robbins' "A White Sport Coat (And a Pink Carnation)."

MOVIES

Your generation's icon of teenage rebellion, James Dean, made only three movies before his untimely death at the age of 24—*East of Eden, Rebel Without a Cause,* and *Giant* (released posthumously).

Once you had a car (or were able to borrow Dad's), drive-in theaters were the place to be—and if yours charged admission by the carload rather than by person, they were cheap, too!

You probably went to a drive-in with your sweetheart to "watch" some of the first-ever movies marketed directly to teens, such as *I Was a Teenage Werewolf, High School Confidential,* or *Gidget.*

Your favorite stars may have included Frank Sinatra, Marilyn Monroe, Marlon Brando, Elvis Presley, Elizabeth Taylor, Rock Hudson, Kim Novak, James Stewart, and John Wayne.

TV

By the mid '50s, Americans were buying an average of 7 million TV sets per year. Approximately one in seven American families owned at least one television, and the typical viewer spent forty-two hours per week watching it.

You probably enjoyed your convenient and modern TV dinners on folding TV tables while watching shows such as *The Red Skelton Hour, I Love Lucy, Gunsmoke, General Electric Theater, American Bandstand,* and *The $64,000 Question.*

You may have even been one of the 30 million viewers to watch the wedding of celebrity actress Grace Kelly to Prince Rainier III of Monaco.

Daniel Marsh, then-president of Boston University, remarked, "If the television craze continues with the present level of programs, we are destined to have a nation of morons." He must not have seen *Rod Sterling and Paddy Chayefsky's Marty*, which is now considered to be the *Citizen Kane* of TV, or Edward R. Morrow's *See It Now*, which did the unthinkable, challenging Senator McCarthy's culture of fear.

SPORTS

. . . .

Mickey Mantle's hallowed Triple Crown season included .340 batting and fifty-two home runs, helping the Yankees clinch the pennant against the Dodgers.

Heavyweight champion Rocky "The Rock" Marciano retired from boxing at the age of 31, undefeated. He won forty-nine fights; all but six of them ended in a KO.

Jim Brown debuted with the Cleveland Browns, leading the league in his first year with 942 yards rushing (including a record-breaking 237 in one game against the Los Angeles Rams).

New York baseball fans lost not one but two teams when longtime rivals the New York Giants and the Brooklyn Dodgers both moved to California.

POP CULTURE

Yours was the first true teenage culture, one marked by
disposable income, sleek automobiles, drive-in theaters and
restaurants, Rock 'n' Roll, rebellion, greasers, preppies,
and beatniks; and often: parental disapproval.

If you were lucky, your first car may have been a Ford
Thunderbird, Chevrolet Corvette, or Cadillac Eldorado.

For fear of a nuclear attack on American soil, roughly one in
twenty families had a fallout shelter in their basement or on their
property. The government encouraged this precaution, circulating
a pamphlet titled "You Can Survive."

Housing developments were everywhere—during 1957, a new
home was built every seven seconds. Despite the sudden recession,
the American dream of home ownership was within reach.

Hopefully, your first car wasn't a Ford Edsel!

IN YOUR 20s

IN THE NEWS

Senator John F. Kennedy, a World
War II hero from a large Irish–Catholic
family, became the 35th President
of the United States.

We gained some ground against the Russians when Alan B.
Shepard became the first American in space—his flight lasted
fifteen minutes. Later, a chimpanzee named Enos circled the
Earth twice for 3 hours and 21 minutes.

After tens of thousands of East German refugees fled to
West Berlin to escape communist rule, the German Democratic
Republic erected a wire fence to divide East Berlin from West.
This simple fence would later become an eleven-foot concrete
barrier known as the Berlin Wall.

In Alabama, racial violence raged: Freedom Riders were
savagely beaten by white mobs in Birmingham, and Martial Law
was declared in Montgomery after a crowd of both adults and
children began throwing stones through the windows of a church
where Dr. Martin Luther King, Jr. was speaking.

The birth control pill gave women the ability to plan or prevent pregnancy, and the Baby Boom came to an end.

EVENTS

· ·

Congress passed the Civil Rights Act, ruling that "discrimination on the basis of sex as well as race in hiring, promoting, and firing," was forbidden.

If you purchased a new car after 1966, it came equipped with seat belts (in all seats) and shatter-resistant windshields. Consumer advocate Ralph Nader's book *Unsafe at any Speed* played a large part in making these safety standards law.

Dr. Christiaan Barnard became a worldwide celebrity when he performed the first successful human heart transplant in Cape Town, South Africa.

Perhaps you were among the 20 million people to take Wednesday off from work to celebrate the first Earth Day. Growing national interest in our environment soon paved the way for the Clean Air and Clean Water Acts.

MUSIC

Back from the Army, Elvis abandoned the youthful rock you once danced to and composed more somber hits like "Don't be Cruel" and "It's Now or Never."

The Beatles made their first-ever American appearance on The Ed Sullivan Show.

When the unique sound of a Motown hit came on your car radio, you couldn't mistake it for anything else. The Detroit label launched the careers of many African American musicians, including The Supremes, whose broad appeal landed them on the top of the Billboard charts twelve times.

Revolutionary music—such as John Lennon's "Give Peace a Chance," James Brown's "(Say It Loud) I'm Black and I'm Proud," or Creedence Clearwater Revival's "Fortunate Son"—both reflected and fueled the times. Perhaps Bob Dylan said it best: "You better start swimming or you'll sink like a stone, for the times they are a-changin.'"

MOVIES

Breakfast at Tiffany's, based on a novella by Truman Capote, made Audrey Hepburn a star and influenced women's fashion nearly as much as Mrs. Kennedy's suits and pillbox hats. (The theme song, "Moon River," also won a Grammy.)

Popular movies of your early 20s included *West Side Story, A Raisin in the Sun, Birdman of Alcatraz,* and *To Kill a Mockingbird.*

After three marriages and many movies, larger-than-life actress (and sex symbol) Marilyn Monroe died from an overdose of sleeping pills in her home at the age of 36.

Walt Disney—creator (and voice) of Mickey Mouse, pioneer of the feature-length cartoon and founder of an entertainment empire—died from lung cancer at the age of 65. (Despite persistent rumors that his body was cryonically preserved, his remains were cremated.)

TV

You may have cooked your first omelet after seeing it done on TV. Julia Child made French cuisine accessible and interesting in *The French Chef*, which ran for ten years.

You may have started watching more football when the family purchased a color TV set. The popularity of Sunday football soared once fans could see the color of their team's uniforms, and the Super Bowl was later created to give this growing audience something to cheer for.

Walter Cronkite may have changed your mind about the Vietnam War—his unflinching coverage and scathing commentary on the CBS Evening News influenced mainstream public opinion.

You and one billion other viewers (roughly one-fifth of the entire world's population!) tuned in to watch Neil Armstrong's historic "one small step."

AMERICA SALUTES
FIRST MEN ON THE MOON

ARMSTRONG   COLLINS   ALDRIN
APOLLO XI
JULY 1969

"Winning isn't everything;
it's the only thing!"

VINCE LOMBARDI

SPORTS

· ·

Records were shattered: New York Yankee, Roger Maris, hit his
61st home run against the Boston Red Sox on the final day of
the 162-game season (Babe Ruth's record was 60 home runs in a
154-game season), and Philadelphia Warriors basketball player
Wilt Chamberlain scored a record-setting 100 points in one game
to beat the New York Knicks 169–147.

You knew Cassius Clay to be a brash personality who did exactly
what he wanted, but many boxing fans were stunned when the
world heavyweight champion converted to Islam and changed his
name to "Muhammad Ali."

After a celebrated career that included 536 lifetime home runs
and netting American League MVP three times, Mickey Mantle
announced his retirement.

POP CULTURE

Cookbooks flew off the shelves: *Better Homes and Gardens Nutrition for Your Family, Casserole Cookbook, The Joy of Cooking: New Edition,* and *The Pillsbury Family Cookbook* were all best sellers.

However, given a voice by Betty Friedan's book, *The Feminine Mystique,* many married women began to question or reject the role that popular culture had assigned to them, choosing to go or return to work after their children were born.

You were most likely to name your children Michael, John, David, James, or Robert if boys; for girls: Lisa, Mary, Susan, Karen, or Kimberly.

Minimum wage was $1.25, and the typical household income was approximately $6,000.

WHEN YOU WERE

IN YOUR 30s

IN THE NEWS

. . . .

The New York Times published top-secret documents that detailed U.S. involvement in Vietnam since World War II. Outraged, President Nixon formed a team called the "plumbers unit" to stop future government leaks—this same team would later break into the Watergate Hotel.

The Vietnam War came to a dramatic conclusion as over 1,000 American civilians and nearly 7,000 South Vietnamese refugees were evacuated from the roof of the U.S. Embassy in Saigon over the course of 18 hours.

One day after his inauguration, President Jimmy Carter made good on a campaign promise by extending a presidential pardon to all draft dodgers.

A partial meltdown at a nuclear power plant less than ten miles from Harrisburg, Pennsylvania (and one-hundred miles from Washington, D.C.) caused nationwide panic. Three Mile Island is now cited as the worst nuclear accident in American history.

Mt. St. Helens erupted with a force equal to 27,000 atomic bombs, killing 57 people and sending a 16-mile-high plume of ash as far as Idaho and Montana.

EVENTS

. . . .

Technology seemed to be growing at an unchecked rate: robotic arms began to replace humans on automobile assembly lines, a CAT scan could look inside your head, a space station called "Skylab" was orbiting the Earth, and Intel of California introduced the microprocessor chip.

No advancement was so shocking as the announcement of the world's first baby conceived in vitro. The "test-tube baby" was born to Lesley and John Brown, an otherwise average British couple who suddenly found themselves in the center of a media maelstrom.

Back at home, disposable razors found their way into the bathroom (and landfills), while your new telephone answering machine was there to take a message (on very small cassette tapes).

The fledgling Apple company began to sell their revolutionary Apple II personal computers, based on a design that Steve Jobs and Steve Wozniak developed in their California garage.

MUSIC

It was a time of departures and new directions: The Beatles officially broke up, and Diana Ross parted ways with The Supremes to begin her solo career.

George McCrae's "Rock Your Baby" and The Hues Corporation's "Rock the Boat" kicked off a briefly lived "Disco era," a time marked by lit floors, flashing lights . . . and polyester.

If you saw Elvis's final tour, you were in for quite a spectacle: that white-caped suit, his martial arts moves, those sweaty scarves . . . Elvis died at the age of 42, and only one day later, heartbroken fans had purchased his records by the millions.

The Rock 'n' Roll of your teenage years had evolved—and not quietly. Heavy metal bands Led Zeppelin, AC/DC, Aerosmith, and Van Halen blew out their amps (and your eardrums); innovative rockers The Eagles and Fleetwood Mac changed the musical landscape; punk rockers The Sex Pistols, Patti Smith, The Velvet Underground, and The Ramones spoke directly to your children's teenaged rebellion.

"May the Force be with you."

STAR WARS

MOVIES

· ·

Perhaps *Diamonds Are Forever,* but this James Bond film marked
Sean Connery's last appearance as Agent 007.

If you watched The 45th Annual Academy Awards, you witnessed
the first use of the show as a political platform when Marlon
Brando, winner of Best Actor for *The Godfather,* sent the president
of the National Native American Affirmative Image Committee to
refuse his Oscar.

You couldn't look at pea soup the same way again after seeing
The Exorcist. Arguably the most terrifying horror movie ever made,
its grotesque special effects caused heart attacks in some theaters.

Science fiction and comic book fans were validated at last by
blockbusters like *Superman, Close Encounters of the Third Kind,
Alien, Star Trek: The Motion Picture,* and the granddaddy of
them all: *Star Wars.*

TV

....

After you were inundated with cigarette ads during your childhood and teenage years, the last-ever cigarette commercial was broadcast during Johnny Carson's *Tonight Show*, one minute before new legislation banning them became law.

The television specials you watched, such as *The Selling of the Pentagon, The U.S./Soviet Wheat Deal: Is There a Scandal?,* and *Watergate: The White House Transcripts* painted a revealing portrait of national opinion.

Everyone loved a sitcom: *Three's Company, Laverne and Shirley, Happy Days, Mork and Mindy,* and *M*A*S*H* were all hits.

If you enjoyed *The Mary Tyler Moore Show,* you were not alone— daring for its time, the show about a single professional woman won the Emmy Award for "Outstanding Comedy Series" three years in a row and launched three spin-off series!

"I don't want them to forget Ruth; I just want them to remember me!"

HANK AARON

SPORTS

American swimmer Mark Spitz took home seven gold medals from the 1972 Munich Olympics, setting new world records in all seven events. Thanks to satellite TV, one billion viewers watched this (and the tragic hostage crisis) live.

Billie Jean King scored a victory for women everywhere (and female athletes in particular) when she humbled Bobby Riggs in an exhibition tennis match billed as the "Battle of the Sexes."

Hank Aaron beat Babe Ruth's home run record of 714 on April 8th, 1974. He didn't stop there—Aaron holds a total of 755 career home runs.

Former Olympic champion Leon Spinks challenged Muhammad Ali for the World Heavyweight Title and won it in a split decision. Ali, however, regained the title seven months later.

POP CULTURE

If you moved, a new single-family home may have cost you around $28,900. A promotion at work? Perhaps you financed an Audi for $3,900, or a new Rolls Royce for $29,700.

It was a time of now-familiar firsts: Starbucks opened its first coffee shop in Seattle, and Gloria Steinem published the first issue of feminist magazine Ms.

On the other hand, by the time you turned 30, there were almost 7,000 fast-food restaurants (compared to 3,400 just several years earlier). Is it any wonder that roughly 33 percent of meals were eaten out of the house?

The Disco Era brought flashing lights, spinning mirror balls, and polyester clothes. Perhaps you still have your favorite leisure suit in a closet somewhere?

IN YOUR 40s

IN THE NEWS

The Reagan administration found itself in hot water when an American cargo plane carrying weapons and military supplies intended for Contra guerrillas was shot down and its illegal purpose discovered.

Millions watched in horror as the space shuttle Challenger—whose crew included Christa McAuliffe, a school teacher—exploded moments after takeoff.

No one likes Mondays, but October 19th, 1987, was particularly bad: After several months of record gains, the Dow Jones plummeted 508 points—nearly 23 percent of its total value.

To make reparations for the Japanese-American relocation camps during World War II, Congress began awarding payments of $20,000 to each surviving internee.

Over one million people took to
the streets of New York City
to join the largest anti-nuclear
demonstration in history.

EVENTS

. . . .

Perhaps you (or your children) owned one of the first Apple II computer systems? Soon after its debut, personal computers could be found in many homes. *Time* magazine even revised their "Man of the Year" feature to award the personal computer with "Machine of the Year."

Slain civil rights leader Martin Luther King, Jr. was honored with the dedication of a new national holiday. Initially, only 27 states observed Martin Luther King, Jr. Day.

The wreck of the RMS Titanic was at last found—broken in two and 12,000 feet under the North Atlantic. What you didn't know was that this discovery happened during a top-secret Navy mission to find the remains of two Cold War-era nuclear submarines.

MUSIC

. . . .

If you had $900–$1,000 to burn, you may have purchased a Sony CDP-101—the world's first commercially released CD player.

First featured in a commercial for the California Raisin Industry, four singing raisins spawned four albums, two TV specials, and a host of merchandise. The shriveled superstars are now part of the Smithsonian's permanent collection.

Think the title track to Bruce Springsteen's hit album "Born in the USA" is about American pride? Many did, and still do. However, "The Boss" wrote the song about how shamefully Vietnam veterans were treated after the war ended.

Other familiar hit songs include Duran Duran's "Hungry Like The Wolf," Starship's "We Built This City," and Def Leppard's "Pour Some Sugar On Me" (though by now, you probably found yourself listening more and more to "oldies" stations).

MOVIES

You were just a kid when Mohandas Gandhi was assassinated, but Richard Attenborough's three-hour epic capably filled in the parts you were too young to understand. *Gandhi* swept the Academy Awards, winning nine in total, including "Best Actor" for Ben Kingsley.

Tom Cruise became a heartthrob with *Risky Business*, and *Top Gun* inspired a fashion throwback: leather bomber and aviator jackets were popular again.

Blockbuster popcorn flicks, such as *Raiders of the Lost Ark, Return of the Jedi, Ghostbusters, The Terminator, Back to the Future,* and especially *E.T., the Extra-Terrestrial,* reigned supreme.

"Movie night" didn't always mean going to the theater—all you had to do was rent a VHS tape from the local Ritz Video or Movie Gallery and pop it into your VCR. (Just don't forget to rewind!)

TV

At a time when the sitcom was dead and no successful show featured a black family, the runaway success of *The Cosby Show* was a bit of a surprise. It was the third most popular show in its first year and the most popular show for the next four.

Why go to the mall? The Home Shopping Network gave you the ability to make all of your impulse purchases from the comfort of your home.

The final episode of *M*A*S*H* shattered TV records by drawing 105.97 million viewers. It held this record for 27 years—until 2010's Super Bowl XLIV.

Though they had been around for decades, soap operas—such as *Dallas, Dynasty, Knot's Landing,* and *Falcon Crest*—were suddenly appointment viewing. An estimated two-thirds of all women with access to television watched at least one soap a day.

"There's 57 channels
and nothing on."

BRUCE SPRINGSTEEN

SPORTS

....

The American star of the 1984 Olympic Games in Los Angeles was track-and-field athlete Carl Lewis, who won four gold medals.

If it hadn't yet, the widespread cocaine problem in the mid-80s got your attention when it claimed two athletes: Len Bias, newly drafted by the Boston Celtics, and professional football player Don Rogers.

Before his illegal betting got him ousted from baseball, Cincinnati Reds batter Pete Rose surpassed 4,191 hits to break a record set 57 years earlier by Ty Cobb.

By 1987, 49.5 percent of American homes had cable TV. And the most popular cable channel by far? ESPN, with 60 million subscribers by the end of the decade.

POP CULTURE

The private lives of celebrities were suddenly matters of great interest. Supermarket tabloids—such as *Star, The Globe,* and *The National Enquirer*—sold by the tens of millions.

It's all about you! Self-help books, from *You Can Negotiate Anything* to *Be Happy You Are Loved,* began to fly off the shelves.

Trivial Pursuit was the hot new game, plastic flowers danced to music, New Coke was quickly replaced with Coca-Cola Classic, and Cabbage Patch Dolls were a huge craze.

If your children have had children of their own, your grandsons might be named Michael, Christopher, Matthew, Joshua, or David. Your granddaughters might be named Jessica, Ashley, Amanda, Jennifer, or Sarah.

IN YOUR 50s

IN THE NEWS

• •

Still reeling from race riots after the Rodney King trial just two
years earlier, Los Angeles was rocked by an early morning
earthquake measuring 6.6 on the Richter scale.

**Bill Clinton was the first President born
after World War II and also the first
Democrat to win reelection since FDR
in 1944.**

A historic peace agreement in Northern Ireland promised to end
the terrorism and civil unrest that had plagued the region for more
than eight decades.

Harkening back to *The Chicago Tribune's* gaffe during your
childhood, many news stations prematurely reported Vice
President Al Gore the winner of the 2000 Presidential election.

Y2K

EVENTS

· ·

Once considered a death sentence, continuous research in drugs suppressing the Human Immunodeficiency Virus led to more effective treatments (and longer lives).

Your science fiction dreams (or fears) came true when scientists in Scotland successfully cloned a lamb named Dolly, igniting a worldwide debate about the implications of cloning technology.

Genetic modification allowed farmers to begin growing produce that was larger and more resistant to insecticides, though some scientists worried about the effects that these altered crops could have on the environment.

If you hadn't gotten around to learning how to use a computer, you had even less incentive to do so now: the Y2K Bug threatened to send society back to the 1900s by exploiting an oversight in computers' internal clocks.

MUSIC

· ·

Two familiar bands reunited to release best-selling live albums: The Eagles' *Hell Freezes Over* and Fleetwood Mac's *The Dance* both debuted at number one on the charts.

Elton John rewrote a song that was originally about Marilyn Monroe and performed it at the funeral of Princess Diana. "Candle in the Wind 97" quickly sold 34 million copies, and all proceeds were donated to charity.

Whitney Houston made her big screen debut with Kevin Costner in *The Bodyguard*, and the album (which featured her international chart-topping cover of Dolly Parton's "I Will Always Love You") became the best-selling soundtrack of all time.

Whether or not you listened to them, Los Del Rio's "Macarena," Celine Dion's "My Heart Will Go On," and Ricky Martin's "Livin, La Vida Loca" were on the radio quite a lot.

KEVIN COSTNER
WHITNEY HOUSTON
THE BODYGUARD
ORIGINAL SOUNDTRACK ALBUM

"Life is like a box of chocolates . . ."

FORREST GUMP

MOVIES

· ·

Denzel Washington starred in two landmark films—as the slain civil rights leader in *Malcolm X* and a lawyer who fights to protect the rights of an HIV-positive man in *Philadelphia*.

Everything old was new again. Movies based on the radio and television shows of your youth included *Dennis the Menace, The Shadow,* and *Leave It to Beaver.*

You probably also enjoyed *Thelma and Louise, The Piano,* and the heartrending *Schindler's List,* which earned a staggering twelve Academy Award nominations and six Oscars, including Best Director and Best Picture.

TV

. . . .

After hosting NBC's *The Tonight Show* for thirty years, Johnny Carson retired from late-night television.

Millions watched minute-by-minute televised coverage of scandals—from the O.J. Simpson police chase and trial to the Tonya Harding / Nancy Kerrigan assault, even to charges of infidelity on the part of the President.

Even if you were one of very few people who didn't watch *Seinfeld*, you couldn't escape people quoting it (not that there's anything wrong with that). After nine seasons, more than 30 million people tuned in to watch the series finale.

Nearly 60 percent of Americans spent most evenings on the couch, giving rise to the term "couch potato."

"Married men live longer than single men. But married men are a lot more willing to die."

JOHNNY CARSON

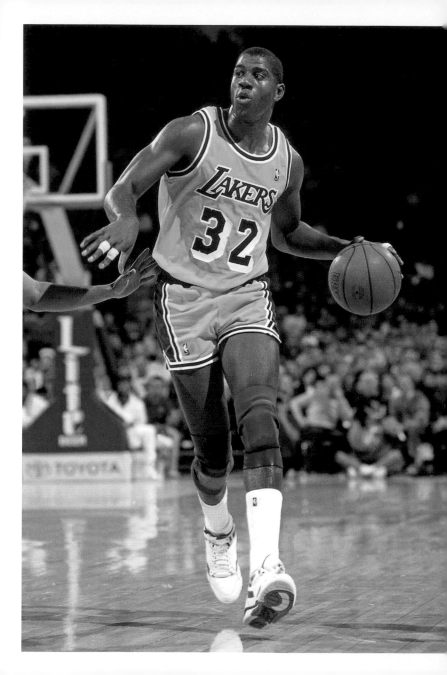

SPORTS

Twenty years after losing the World Heavyweight Title to Muhammad Ali (and after ten years away from heavyweight competitions), George Foreman reclaimed his title by knocking out Michael Moorer in ten rounds.

Basketball fans were stunned when three-time MVP Earvin "Magic" Johnson announced that he was HIV-positive and would retire from the NBA.

After stumbling in two previous Olympic competitions, American speed skater Dan Jensen exemplified perseverance by taking home the gold medal and setting a new world record in the 1994 Winter Olympics' 1,000-meter event.

Baseball fans were not pleased when a 257-day strike led to the cancellation of that year's World Series.

POP CULTURE

· ·

Fanny packs were hip, emoticons put smiles in your e-mail, Beanie Babies were must-have collectibles, books on tape let you read while driving, and you learned that *Men Are from Mars, Women Are from Venus.*

Dr. Deepak Chopra may have changed your mind about Alternative Medicine with his best-selling book *Ageless Body, Timeless Mind.* If so, you weren't alone—*Time* magazine even named Chopra one of the Top 100 Icons and Heroes of the Century.

Little John-John, or John F. Kennedy, Jr., was now "the world's sexiest man," but no longer a bachelor—his marriage to Carolyn Bessette made headlines.

You weren't imagining it: Popular culture seemed obsessed with youth as advertisers trained their sights almost exclusively on your grandchildren and their friends. By the late '90s, teens were 31 million strong and willing to spend most of their money on music and movies.

Men Are from Mars, Women Are from Venus.

AUTHOR JOHN GRAY

IN YOUR 60s

IN THE NEWS

No one expected the devastation of Hurricane Katrina. The Category Four storm claimed the lives of nearly two thousand New Orleans natives and the homes of many more.

The space shuttle Columbia unexpectedly disintegrated after its return from a successful 16-day mission. All seven astronauts were killed, and debris from the shuttle rained across hundreds of miles of Texas countryside.

From Mr. Universe to the Terminator to . . . California's 38th Governor? After surprising the world by announcing his candidacy on *The Tonight Show with Jay Leno*, voters elected Arnold Schwarzenegger over 134 other candidates.

When you heard the news, you probably thought it was a practical joke: Pluto is no longer considered a planet.

September 11th, 2001. We will never forget.

EVENTS

. . . .

Previously a bulky thing for affluent people (or show-offs),
the cell phone evolved by leaps and bounds.

Were you one of 50 million people without power during the
Northeast Blackout of 2003? After a cascading power failure,
eight U.S. states and parts of Canada were left without electricity
for a day or longer.

A massive earthquake measuring 9.0 on the Richter scale loosed
a disastrous tsunami on Southeast Asia, killing over 225,000 and
displacing 1.2 million more.

From humble beginnings to 44th
President of the United States,
Barack Obama showed the world
that the American dream is very
much alive.

MUSIC

The way people listen to music has changed just as much as the music itself: from LPs to 8-tracks and then cassette tapes to CDs and finally to portable MP3 players like the Apple iPod, which can easily hold your entire music library.

With the option to buy music online by the song or album, digital downloads eclipsed sales of the physical CD. Tower Records, Virgin Records, and hundreds of independent record stores across the country began closing their doors.

Alicia Keys was a piano-playing phenomenon, releasing four albums (including her runaway sophomore hit, "The Diary of Alicia Keys") and stacking up twelve Grammy Awards.

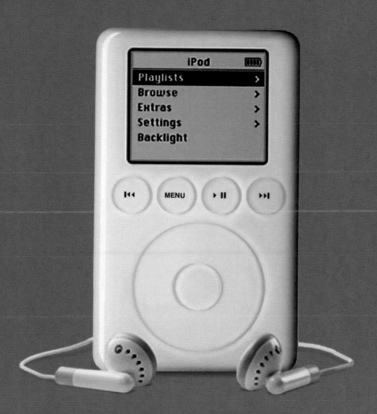

MOVIES

· ·

Audrey Tautou swept you away in *Amélie*, a fairy tale-like love story set in Paris. Even if you don't like reading subtitles, you're probably glad you made an exception.

Good Night, and Good Luck portrayed the "McCarthyism" of your early teenage years through the eyes of Edward R. Murrow and his producer Fred W. Friendly.

Whether you read the books when they were first published or just remember seeing "Frodo Lives!" on buttons and T-shirts later on (and wondering what it meant), no one would deny that Peter Jackson's massively epic (and epically massive) *Lord of the Rings* film trilogy was the movie event of the decade.

Thanks to her powerful performance in *Monster's Ball,* Halle Berry became the first African–American woman to win an Academy Award for "Best Actress."

TV

· ·

Remember when television sets were built into really heavy wooden cabinets? Flat-screen TVs are so light that they can be mounted on your wall.

You may have grown up watching *Candid Camera,* but mega-popular shows such as *Survivor, American Idol,* and *The Apprentice* seem to bear little resemblance to the "Reality TV" of your youth.

You had to spring for the premium cable package (or wait for the DVDs) to catch some of the best shows on television, such as *The Sopranos, Six Feet Under, The Wire, The Shield,* and one that is certain to bring back some memories—*Mad Men.*

If you watched CNN's coverage of the 2008 Presidential elections, you may have seen something right out of the science fiction movies of your drive-in days: a live hologram image of a reporter from Chicago beamed into a studio in New York.

"You're Fired!"

DONALD TRUMP

SPORTS

Long-beleaguered Boston Red Sox fans had their day when their team beat the St. Louis Cardinals to win their first World Series Championship in eighty-six years.

NASCAR fans were stunned when seven-time Winston Cup champion Dale Earnhardt suffered a fatal crash during the final lap of the Daytona 500.

American cyclist Lance Armstrong survived cancer to take home seven Tour de France titles—and counting!

American swimmer Michael Phelps won eight events at the 2008 Beijing Olympics, setting a new record for the most gold medals won in a single Olympics.

POP CULTURE

· ·

Perhaps you have wondered why celebrities your age are starting to look younger than you do? In many cases, the answer is Botox injections, which temporarily paralyze certain facial muscles, smoothing wrinkles and creating a more youthful (if somewhat puffy) face.

Contemporary fashion has taken a cue from previous decades—"vintage" items such as cocktail and sheath dresses as well as men's blazers have become popular with today's youth. (Could it be that they do listen to their elders . . . ?)

If your grandchildren have recently become parents, they most likely named your great-grandchildren Jacob, Michael, Ethan, Joshua, or Daniel if boys; for girls: Emma, Isabella, Emily, Madison, or Ava.

Facebook:

A new way to keep in touch with family, friends, and people you've lost track of over the years.

NOW

MOST PEOPLE YOUR AGE ARE:

- Currently married and homeowners.
- Retired and able to spend more time with family.
- Living in Florida, Pennsylvania, or West Virginia.
- Spending their days socializing, reading, taking medications, watching TV, praying, and driving.
- Not using the Internet on a daily basis, if at all.
- Less affected by current financial conditions than their children.
- Unconvinced of the necessity of a cell phone.
- Feeling younger than their age!

LOOK WHO ELSE IS IN THEIR 70S:

- Ann-Margret, Actress
- Rev. Jesse Jackson, Activist
- Pete Rose, Baseball Player and Manager
- Martha Stewart, Entrepreneur
- Al Pacino, Actor
- Chubby Checker, Musician
- Tom Brokaw, Journalist
- Sue Grafton, Author
- Don Imus, Radio Personality
- Nancy Pelosi, former U.S. Speaker of the House
- Sir Patrick Stewart, Actor
- Muhammad Ali, Heavyweight Boxer
- Stephen Hawking, Physicist
- Aretha Franklin, Musician
- Garrison Keillor, Radio Personality
- Paul Simon and Art Garfunkel, Musicians

**IF YOU HAVE ENJOYED THIS BOOK,
WE WOULD LOVE TO HEAR FROM YOU.**

Please send your comments to:
Hallmark Book Feedback
P.O. Box 419034
Mail Drop 215
Kansas City, MO 64141

Or e-mail us at:
booknotes@hallmark.com